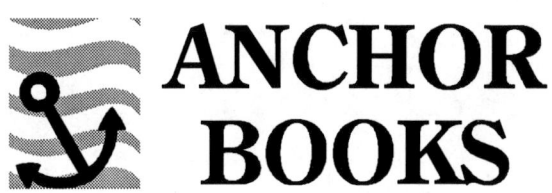

ANCHOR BOOKS

CELEBRATIONS IN VERSE FROM THE NORTH

Edited by

Neil Day

First published in Great Britain in 2001 by
ANCHOR BOOKS
Remus House,
Coltsfoot Drive,
Peterborough, PE2 9JX
Telephone (01733) 898102

HB ISBN 1 85930 951 8
SB ISBN 1 85930 956 9

FOREWORD

Anchor Books is a small press, established in 1992, with the aim of promoting readable poetry to as wide an audience as possible.

We hope to establish an outlet for writers of poetry who may have struggled to see their work in print.

The poems presented here have been selected from many entries. Editing proved to be a difficult task and as the Editor, the final selection was mine.

I trust this selection will delight and please the authors and all those who enjoy reading poetry.

Neil Day
Editor

CONTENTS

LIFE IS FEEDING THE BIRDS

I threw some crumbs today
And from all around
I could feel their joyous interest
They sang in unfriendly bare twigged trees
They swooped down from unseen hidden places
And for just one short moment
I shared their gratefulness
They were thankful for just another meal
And lived in that moment
From meal to meal
Not knowing when it might come
Or from where
But they thanked the moment
They lived the moment to capacity
And were happy
The instance soon passed
In looking for more sustenance
For their busy existence battles on for survival
But that friendly moment, is never lost
Cheekily pecking, playfully nibbling
Their chirpy wide-eyed innocence
Viewing me with a friendly caution
As if to say
'Thank you my friend for my food today'
And they continue to eat
As if only to make *me* happy
I threw the bread
Small crumbs of life
And got in return
Abundant life.

Kathleen Thacker

BLACKTHORN IN WINTER WOOD

The sun on that splendid day
Shone brighter than I have ever seen before,
Mary took Blackthorn on display
Between the bramble and thickets galore.
Across the meadows they together traced
A tireless path of stamina and youth,
Down past the woodlands they raced
As if in eagerness they strove at truth.
Along the brook side path they roamed
Where pebbles danced loose and free,
It was there that Blackthorn gave that awful moan
And stumbled to the wayside helplessly.
Three years have passed silently by
Blackers has long since stilled,
Mary holds absence of the eye
Away until that vacated place is filled.
It was as the winter wood slowly burned
A flame for my entranced stare,
That my thoughts wayward turned,
To catch a fleeting glance of that much-missed mare.

Mark Atkinson

UNTITLED

So many smiles to hide the pain,
So much trying with so little gain,
So much laughter to hide the fear,
So much 'fun' to hide the tears,
So much nonsense to hide from the truth.

So much sighing and wishing and wasting,
Not enough forgetting, ignoring and getting;
Striving for something I know not what without
taking a proper look at what I've got.
Not enough appreciating, thanking, enjoying -
wanting what can't be found is slowly destroying.

Angie Waller

UNLOCKED BEAUTY

O solitude, within this serene bower I with thee dwell,
    The moon has hung her lamp on high
    And pass'd in radiance through the cloudless sky,
The sweet sky seemed not far above,
    Adorned with beauty and boundless eyes
    In rapturous silence like spiritual brides,
Tall and erect, with milk-white clusters hung,
    Lovelier and sweeter with arms of might,
    Proud oak stands in the blue of the night.

The spirit of enjoyment and desire
    Soon did this place become my other home,
    My dwelling, my heaven, my very own,
There is eminence in the stars tonight
    Above me and so distant in the clear blue sky,
    All things from heaven are hallow'd and high,
In the vast firmament the moon like to a silver bow
    Cold and fruitless in the virgin morn,
    Like a royal monarch, to the palace born.

Warm in her breast, earth drinks the dew,
    The corn is green, and hawthorn buds appear,
    Earth will unfold another year,
My conscious heart will breathe with just applause,
    This unlocked beauty with magic powers
    With majestic robes in virgin bowers,
God's earth has never seemed so fair
    Nor any of his creatures so divine,
    O moon tell me why there must be, a parting time.

John Leighton

PAIN

I've been up a mountain,
I've been down a cave,
Danced all night to the local rave,
I've walked on hot sand
With my heart on my hand,
But never have I suffered such pain.

I've ridden on a shire,
Walked in the mire,
A rifle I learned how to fire,
And the pain it was shocking,
Never have I suffered such pain.

I've walked till I've dropped,
My ears they have popped,
When gazing in awe
At the view from the top,
But never have I suffered such pain.

With my car on the blink,
I need time to think,
But the pain, such pain,
Is driving me insane,
Never have I suffered such pain.

I can't sleep at night,
I must look a sight,
And the pain, such pain,
Is making me lame,
But never have I suffered such pain.

I'm a wreck, a twisted wreck,
My smile now a grimace,
I've only myself to blame,
But never have I suffered such pain.

Sue Peach

A SOLDIER'S CRY

The earth so silent, as with breath held tight
Men awaiting the passing of so long a night
Ears strained for the sound none wished to hear
Hearts torn asunder, the waiting drear
As all about nerves taught with fear

The trumpet blast froze every heart
As to the ramparts men made a start
None quite sure of why or wherefore
Only that that's what they were there for

The morn now rent, with cannon's roar
As trumpet orders, *'Charge'* to the fore
Forward they go through bullets whistling
To the screams of dying friends not listening

Then one man feels that fatal ball
That his life force does let spill out
Face turned skyward his anguished voice we hear
My God, oh my God, why was I here?

Then down on cool accepting earth he lies
Softer and softer sound those fearsome cries
Now in that vale of peace he lay
As face to the morning sun; he passed away.

George Ball

THE DOLLS' HOUSE

Let's spring clean and wash and dust,
Make sure the floors have all been brushed.
Light the fire so bright to see,
Set the table for our tea.
Bring the candles and a cake,
And I will see what I can bake.
When our house is spic and span,
We'll invite the pedlar man.
We'll ask him what is on his tray,
That we may like to buy today.
Flowers and beads and bells perhaps,
Ribbons and trims and pin to match.
Magic pens, invisible inks,
Primrose scents and garden pinks.
I'll buy a jar of honey or two,
One for me and one for you.
We'll have a lovely time, you'll see,
When the dolls' house pedlar comes to tea.

Irene Moor

TIME GOES BY

Time goes by stealing each season:
each season goes by fading in time,
love goes by without rhyme nor reason,
rhyme nor reason making love mine,
spring's sweet sensual moment's saved me,
summer forever so it seemed,
autumn golden treasure I gave thee,
winter my love 'twas redeemed,
lost in the year's we neglected,
found with a moment to spare,
your fate with mine 'tis connected,
this imperfect world we must share,
    where love's precious gifts, are forgiving,
    true love is for life, with this life then for living.

Joseph Finlow

SUBMISSION

So we meet again; your perseverance is beyond belief.
An insistent caller, determined to wheedle your way into my affections.
Soliciting attention; hoping that my defences will be down -
    You resolute and *daring* schemer.

How plaintive your cry, how defiant your resolve.
Did not my last rejection hold some sway in your consciousness?
Were you unaware that your presence was at that time unwanted -
    You pitiful, but brave intruder into my home?

Your rejection of solitude, your desire for comfort and love;
In-built sureties for a quality of life worth having.
I respect and understand the needs intrinsic to your existence -
    Most noble and distinguished beast.

Now, your magnetic gaze is enough to make me change my mind;
Your confident and discriminate choice shows attributes most worthy.
Oh feline being, oh silent prowler, make my home yours -
    You amorous and sensuous creature.

Wendy Kirkpatrick

PHENOMENON

A blinding moment that can reveal
A prelude to dawn a prelude to night
Part of nature's artwork and yet surreal
But is half dark or is half light?

For with the speed of Muhammed Ali
The world is suspended in sharp relief
The melting clocks of Salvador Dali
For that second aren't beyond belief

It's similar to a flash of lightning
As if for a time the world had lost its way
On both your hands the knuckles whitening
But why this happens you cannot say

Only for a moment it's here and gone
Have you ever caught this phenomenon?

John Smurthwaite

PLANET EARTH

Surrounded by a billion stars
that could have planets like our own
we reside amongst the Milky Way
in a galaxy, here on Earth, which is our home.

In the vast depths of space too far to see
are trillions of galaxies where life could possibly be
so many, if each were a grain of sand
they would fill up the beaches on all our land.

To see Earth from space is a beautiful sight
reflecting the sunlight its colours so bright
the blues of the oceans, greens and browns of the land
the whites of the clouds, all created by a powerful hand.

The wonders of nature, the magic of spring
when plants re-awake, life anew for everything
the richness of summer, the colours of flowers
it's hard to believe that all this is ours!

In the autumn red and brown leaves start to fall
yellows and golds of the foliage makes us wonder at it all
then in the winter, so peaceful, Mother Nature goes to sleep
and builds up her strength, the next year's promise to keep.

The mysteries of the heavens are many
prompting scientists around the world to converse
time and space is so vast and intriguing
slowly, man learns the secrets of the universe.

We must look after our planet and treat it with love
given so many blessings from the Almighty above
respect your surroundings and consider their worth
this gem in space irreplaceable, the beautiful 'planet Earth'!

Tony W Rylatt

OUR MERSEY

Fast flowing Mersey, how long have you been gushing
From Stockport to Liverpool; never pausing, always rushing
Through Altrincham, Boden and Hale, what lovely memory
Could you recollect. What panoramic scenes of beauty

Sometimes you run slow, sometimes you run fast
Wave as you pass Thelwall, a city from the past
By Irlam, Woolston Weir and on past Paddington
We see you rush 'neath Kingsway Bridge and onto Howley Quay

Onward Mersey ancient river, such changes you have seen
Thames Board Mills and Crosfields, replacing land so green
Twisting and winding past Fiddlers Ferry
Through Widnes so fast, a river so smelly
Joined in its rushing, its flowing, its haste
By industrial pollution and toxicated waste

Past Liverpool Docks where ships sail unfurled
Laden with cargo they travelled the world
Goodbye to those places, hello to the sea
Oh Mersey! Keep flowing, long after me.

Gordon R Cooper

A MOTHER'S LOVE

It was never the beatings she gave me
That caused me pain.
The large hands raised high above my head,
The blows that rained down on my body
Like the sting of hail.
It was her disappointment in me
That I wore like a cloak,
That covered me from head to toe,
That weighed my body down.
The knife edged tongue,
The bitter words that slashed me to the bone,
And when she died, sympathetic people would say
'You must miss your mother.'
'Yes,' I would reply, 'I've missed her all my life.'

Christine A Flinn

LOWRY'S PEOPLE

Along the high streets,
the glass covered arcades
of northern towns.
The same people, lonely
solitary figures; scurry,
hastening to an unknown
destination, a meeting,
a rave-up, early tea and TV!
Children hurry to absenteeism
in some crowded mall;
where oldies sit, staring
vacantly, daydreaming.
Slum tenements have gone,
replaced by high rise,
awaiting demolition
and the matchstick men and women
still have their worries,
their fears; in a still
far from ideal world.

R E Fairclough

THE CRUEL SEA

I pray each night for those in peril on the sea
Sailing far away on the deep ocean who never foresee
The dangers, those who man the trawlers so sleek
In all weathers to bring home food for us to eat
The lifeboat crew who devote their time and lives
To save others in order that they will survive
When the cruel sea appears so hungry
Causing hazards and havoc to all and sundry
Sailing through hell but they carry on
Battling the elements, never hesitating until their mission is done.
The calling and passion one has to sail the deep ocean
A feeling to venture over the high seas is quite an emotion,
A challenge to sail around the globe maybe is a joy
For those drawn to the cruel sea whether girl or boy
To view the waters around the world's tropical isles
Where perhaps the sea is sombre and more docile
Breathing in clear fresh sea air
Forgetting how cruel that sea can be elsewhere
When the turbulent waves rage at night
Lashing and tossing everything in sight.
Gnawing at the earth's deep vaults
Forcefully pouring into crevices, just one big somersault
Those giant waves like high mountains
And the spray cascading into enormous fountains
Eroding away the earth and rocks
Crumbling them into shingles on the seashore and docks,
Until perhaps one day it will take over for evermore
When history repeats maybe as in the times of Noah
The meeting of the tides which turn like heaven and hell
But our trust in the Good Lord will depend on his love
we all know so well.

Nancy Owen

TREES

Nature's fingers
  stretching skywards,
Scrubbing air
  with verdant touch.

Graceful columns
  standing proudly,
Supporting beds
  for weary clouds.

Ringed with age
  they stand aloof,
Stately homes
  for feathered families.

Bowing low
  to wind's advances,
They are larynx
  to wind's voice.

Resting finally
  at life's long end,
To haunt the page
  beneath these words.

John S Davies

IN OUR ATTIC

I went up in our attic
Climbing every creaking stair
And looked for hidden treasure
That I knew was waiting there
But then I started screaming
It echoed through the house
Instead of finding golden coins
I found a little mouse.

Kerrie-Jo Gleave (11)

I WON'T CONFORM

Quietly, silently I'll conform,
Don't honour my protest,
Just fill in the form.

Quietly, silently hear me weep,
Don't honour my protest,
Just stand and peep.

Quietly, silently pollute the air,
Don't honour my protest,
Just sit on this chair.

Quietly, silently see me stand,
Don't honour my protest,
Just listen to the band.

Quietly, silently watch me write,
Don't honour my protest,
Just fade into night.

Quietly, silently I'll sit and stare,
Don't honour my protest,
Just show me you care.

Quietly, silently I won't conform,
Don't honour my protest,
Just rip up the form.

C Todd

LINE DANCING

Good line dancers
Few and far between
Weekly sessions
At the Queen's.

Big Jim our teacher
Always there
Helping hand
To learn, share.

Experience dances
Fun, pleasure.
Everybody gathers together
Nights remembering
All you're taught.

Tush push, cha-cha
East coast swing
Different temp
Make dance sing.

Music fast
Music slow
Jim does not mind
How you go.

Hat, boots, tassels, things
Fancy shirts, skirts
Colours bright
Swishing, swaying
Through the night.

Costume Style
Country way
Beautiful watching
Any day.

Gail Rowan

DOUBTS

Slowly the evangelist faced each one
Gently prodded each shoulder to demand
Are you a Christian?
Each one fervently replied, 'I am.'
Not me, shamed and reluctant, 'I try.'
So many years have passed yet still
My questions are not resolved.
The everlasting 'why?', too much sorrow
Too much evil, inhumanity.
Is it too late to try again
And say with faith, hope and love
'Yes, I am.'

C Shepherd

WONDERFUL THINGS
(The Gift)
(In memory of Baz)

To awake with the birds on a summer's morn and see the delights of nature unfold with the growing warmth of the rising sun, is indeed a wonderful thing. To be blessed with the gift of sight, sound and smell is a wonderful thing. Such simple things that enable me to see the colours in nature's creations, to hear the song of nature's creations and to smell the oh so sweet aroma of nature herself; things forever present, but often unseen and untouched by those who have lost the 'Gift.' A wonderful thing is the 'Gift.' Oh what a wonderful thing life could be if only we would let it. Instead, we choose to squabble and fight with our fellow inhabitants of God's planet and it is at such times that people lose the 'Gift.' For some of the people the 'Gift' is restored and cherished forever more. But, more often than not, the 'Gift' is lost forever and to those who have lost it, a great burden is placed upon their shoulders - a burden which will remain, no matter how many tears are shed in regret.

The 'Gift' is a wonderful thing; but it can only remain so, for as long as it is treated with the respect it deserves.

It is said that a man who loses sight of the 'Gift' shall be granted a life-long companionship with his creator's foe. My advice is simple: Wherever life may take you, be sure to take the 'Gift' with you, for if you don't, you may just find yourself in a hot-house . . .

Margaret Turrell

MY MERMAID

I saw a mermaid out at sea,
I know you will laugh at me.
She dived down into the ocean blue.
In her dive she took a spin
Too late to correct, so she couldn't swim.

Suddenly upon the seashore of pure white sand
Lay my mermaid without a sound.
Is she alive or will she die?
Open your eyes and let me see,
So I can tell the world of your beauty.
Palm trees sway on a gentle breeze,
Was it a dream or was it real?

Her tail shone of shades of blue,
No not really, maybe a green hue!
Scales of silver then of gold,
Should I touch? No I'm not that bold.
Suddenly a sound is heard
With a flick of her tail
She dived into the ocean blue.
Was she a dream, or was she true?
This is where I'll leave it to you.

Elizabeth A Wilkinson

MY DEAR CHILD

The day that you were born,
was the best day of my life.
I held you in my arms
and watched you smile.
You were so beautiful
lying there, so pure, so innocent.
The pain I'd felt had now all gone
I cried, though I wasn't sad.
I checked your toes, your fingers, your body,
it was perfect,
just like you.
I stroked your hair,
and kissed you for the very first time.
Wrapped in a blanket, you were warm and safe
and that's the way you'll stay,
warm and safe,
my dear child.

Joanne Gilbertson

CHASING LOVE AWAY

The carpets still harbour their dust
I long to find some of your scales
Some of your skin
But the vacuum's on hold
And the fears grow deeper within
The plaster on the walls
cease to hold back the world outside
The cracks can no longer hide
The bareness of the stone
The barrenness of my life
since you've been gone
The roof clasps me as an umbrella
But the nails are still raw
Sharp, pointed, stained with sorrow
Happiness is just a word
Devoid of all emotion
It savours its unwillingness to deliver
My ears are now my enemy
They enhance the silence, the deafening silence
The windows just stare back
Their portraits of another world left behind
Summer, winter, spring, autumn
Who cares - since you've been gone
The mirror no longer smiles back
It hangs disdainfully, full of self-pity
Instead of remorse
Thank God you left the clock
It talks to me sweetly
But unconvincingly
Its parched echoes deadening the
Numbness that surrounds me
My landscape has changed
Where tears fall into waterfalls

And dreams smother
The smoothest of memories
Hanging, clinging, entwining in desperation
Thirsty for an even greater hunger
To charge their inner belief in survival
The pillows absorb my tears
Sometimes they swallow my fears
Of living without you.

Mike Hynde

As I Lie Awake

Though sleeping hours are here once more
I'm wakeful, as the night before
I'm so content, here next to you
Sleep, stay away - you'll spoil the view
I lie in watch - behold your grace
I stroke your hair - caress your face
I watch you rest in sleeping peace
And feel your breath - a soothing breeze
I can't describe my heartfelt love
Where could I start? Words aren't enough
Just read my heart and then you'll know
You are my world - I love you so
These moments mean so much to me
I bless this prized serenity
I celebrate each breath you take
And love you as I lie awake . . .

John Hartley

OUR FEATHERED FRIENDS

I watch the little sparrows as they flitter to and fro,
In and out of the bushes they quickly come and go.
Feeding from the table or down upon the ground,
But easily frightened by any little sound.
Along comes the robin, the guardian of the patch
He thinks it is his duty the sparrows to despatch.
Busily he inspects his spot, then checks the seeds are in his pot.
Then Mrs Blackbird comes along, while Mr sits and sings his song.
There's plenty of bread upon the ground, more than enough to
go around.
Time for the starlings to arrive for a feed,
They scatter the sparrows in their haste and their greed.
They quarrel and fight and jostle and shout,
Finding the best morsel is what it's all about.
Nothing left now lying around, just a few crumbs upon the ground.
Must quickly replace the fat balls and seed,
For soon the tit families will be here to feed.
Dusk has arrived, all is now still, our Feathered Friends have
eaten their fill.
Tucked in their nests and out of sight,
All safely roosting for the night.

Joan P Mayer

GRIEVING

I feel so alone, empty inside
The night you left I sat and cried
I could not believe you'd leave me this way
Oh God, I wish, let him stay one more day

I close my eyes, your face I can see
I want to touch, I want to be,
beside you tonight when I fall asleep
I don't want to wake up and start to weep

I miss your smell, I miss your voice
Please God, will you give me a choice?
Of turning the clock back and starting again
Let me feel happy, take away this pain

My body is filled with so much sorrow
At this moment in time there is no tomorrow
The voice inside me starts to scream
Let me wake up and find it a dream

Death, it says, comes to us all
And while we are here we should have a ball
But to take you away at such a young age
I think of God and I fill up with rage.

Alison Robinson

HUNGER

In far away places hundreds of children will die,
Lying helpless and starving no tears left to cry,
But why does this happen
No food or no rain,
All around us such sorrow, but who is to blame?

Moms cradle their babies just praying they'll live,
But water and food they're unable to give,
In their arms they are dying, but what can they do
And we sit here moaning, we haven't a clue?

As we are so lucky we have all that we need,
But we still want lots more, we are filled with such greed,
So next time you're moaning I'm hungry, I'm cold,
Well just think to yourself
At least I'll grow old.

Please think how those mothers are feeling today,
Their anger and pain, it won't go away.
'Cause they've lost their babies
But what can they do?
Then we say we've got nothing, we haven't a clue.

Mandi Edkins

IN MEMORY OF LUCKY MY CAT

My cat, my cat, my black and white cat,
Lucky was her name.
She would run and bounce about
And play funny games.
She was friendly and faithful too,
I often told her that I love you.
Lucky was thirteen and passed away,
I'll never forget that sad, sad day.
We'll love her and miss her forever more,
Now she's with Cindy, together they'll explore,
The fields are green, the gates are gold
Up in Heaven, Lucky and Cindy, so very bold.

Gillian Corbett

SUMMER SON

You are like the sun, the only one,
and whenever we entwine
the sun can only shine.
To dream without a care -
spells are dancing in the air.
Dancing to a different tune
when you walked into my rune.
You who captured my dreams
who lives in separate realms.
With the fire and life in my heart
gone, two worlds apart -
With the light from my very eyes,
like the fiery sun in the skies.
Dimension number three
is being here with me.
Vines entwined by hearts and mind
spiritual flow in a golden glow -
Summer heat and summer love,
feels like forever is rising above -
Fantasies of far away lands,
exotic music and salty sands.
It was always meant to be you, it was always me,
Remember that maybe the future's not yours to see
I hold the key
to the truth inside of me.
You speak to me and my soul
shines like the sun.
Rising with the love that burns
for the only one.

Amanda A B Sherry

ANOTHER BIRTHDAY

Birthday presents
heaped on the floor
remind her that
another year
has passed.

The cards wishing
her 'all the best',
telling her how
old she is now,
in verse.

Memories jogged,
previous years,
cake with candles,
they all joined in
to sing.

Not this year though,
she sits alone,
gifts all opened,
what a present
old age.

Telephone rings,
dark clouds lifted,
bustle about,
prepare some tea
for guests.

Visitors gone,
time to reflect -
friends, family,
'Happy Birthday'
hopes met.

Angela Pritchard

SHOOTING STAR

The sleep that would not take my eyes
Led me to the darkened skies
To see a single path of light
Live but for a second's flight.
Wandering matter caught
In gravitational pull
Plunging down but not to land
Except as dust.

Restless, unable to sleep
I rise to gaze upon the moon.
A single trace of light
Arcs across the sky
Adding to the myriad specks
Of other ill begotten treks.
Oh could that I
But follow that glowing track
To sleep.

Burning through the atmosphere
I did not hear you cry at all
So fast was your fevered fall
So quick the sear into oblivion.
My eye-blink missed the moment
You disappeared
To lie as dust, asleep.
Yet for anther's death, I weep.

John Aldred

LABYRINTH

There are no walls, no fences, and no bars
In fact there are no physical barriers at all
But it's there as real as any prison
A structure so complicated, escape seems impossible
I can sense it all around, mocking me
Waiting for me to make a bid for freedom
And when I think I have unlocked its secrets
It draws me back in with unseen hands
I seem helpless against its power
I pray for inner strength to aid my salvation
But there is only heartache and despair
Is there to be no respite from my torment
Is this to be my destiny for eternity?
No! I refuse to give in I must have faith
One day I will conquer the labyrinth
One day *I shall be free*

Thomas Carey

TO BE A WRITER

To be a writer, that's what I aspire to be,
That means I'll seek out any opportunity,
To put my thoughts down - no matter what!
Sometimes it's convenient, sometimes it's not.
What I really find hard to understand,
Is they don't come when they're planned.
Sometimes I can sit and sit and sit,
Staring at paper with not a word on it.
Poised, with pen in hand, ready to go,
Ready to jot down an abundant flow!
Hours later after waiting like this,
I decide I'll give it a miss.
I set about doing other things.
You can guess what that brings!
'Quick, where's the paper and the pen,
The thoughts are coming once again.'
Why didn't they come when I wanted them to?
Why arrive when there's lots else to do?
Most of the time it's not that way.
I can usually write what I want to say,
There's times when I take up my pen,
Thinking I'll add to my book once again.
I can't seem to settle into doing it,
Thoughts that rhyme come bit by bit.
Maybe that's not what I choose,
But either way what can I lose?
Words should be used to bring pleasure,
Containing encouragement as their treasure.
They should bring sunshine into a day,
When people relate to what they say.
That's the kind of writing for me,
The kind of writer I intend to be.

Rosina L Gutcher

ARCHAEOLOGIST

You found me
prostrate beneath
a condemned hotel.
Dusting my shoulder
with the care of a woman
forming her cheeks
exposing ribs
or fingers
you could not be sure

I grimaced in
the first sunlight
for centuries
sheltering my sunken eyes
in an armpit
'Take me away'
I willed you -
'preserve me behind glass
on the pedestal
of your museum'

Mark Griffiths

AND LEFT THE VIVID AIR SIGNED WITH THEIR HONOUR

They were so young
And barely trained,
They came to War
As their country claimed,

'Twas but a game
They had to play
And win or lose
Their life that way.

Their honour was
The bond they made
When at last
They made the grade.

The odds against
Their safe return
They understood but said 'Not me,
The others, will not burn!'

Until one night, the target dead ahead,
They too became just one more thing
To feature in the News we read:
'Some of our aircraft are missing!'

Stanley T Harpham
(Sgt. Pilot, RAF, 2nd World War)

THE CHILDREN

I heard the voices again
Children's voices, subdued sometimes
Sometimes giggling
As if they were hiding from one another.
Then calling to one another
'Where are you?'
'I can't find you!'
'Come out, wherever you are.'

The room was full of sunshine
Dust floating on the beams of light
As the wood in the old house
Settled in the warm sun.

I hear them running downstairs
And I step into the hall
'Who are you?' I ask
And there is silence.

I can feel their presence
As though they watch me.
Then I hear their voices again
Giggling and laughing together.

As they run back upstairs
Their footsteps echoing
In the quiet house
Then all is still again.

The past is ever with us
As is the future
And one is enfolded in the other
Time is but a measure.

The happiness of the boys
Enfolds me
Are they in a time warp?
Or just shadows that come and go.

I will never know
Because I have to move on
To create my own impressions
Or shadows to leave behind.

Joan May Wills

CHRIST IS BORN

Sweet infant holy,
Sweet infant lowly,
Bright star of morning brings the dawn.
Sleep gently holds Him,
Beauty enfolds Him,
Loving arms cradle free from harm.

Soon comes the morrow
Laden with sorrow.
Soon come the heartache, darkness and scorn.
Soon comes the smiter,
Piercing and bitter,
Soon comes the nail, the crown of cruel thorn.

Shepherds adore Him
Bow down before Him,
Angels in Heaven hail the morn.
Bells boldly ringing,
Choirs gaily singing,
Glad tidings bringing,
Christ is born!

John M Beazley

SILKEN SILENCE

The silken gauze of bold contempt
Once hid us from the prying eye
Now hangs in shreds,
Ravaged by the moths of time.
And we - in meeting thus,
Now stand exposed,
Our quiet discourse
Once silenced in the noisy air
The ever anxious ears invade
When you and I are side by side.

These whispered moments,
In a crowded room
Can be no more.
And we, some other screen must weave
To shield us from the glassy stare,
Proud victims of sick gossip's fare
That burns the lamp,
Not light to give
But darkened corners darker make.
They whose tongues are living death
Know not the pleasure of sweet breath
That whispers.

M R Mackinnon-Pattison

SHE

Time has her strong fingers round my throat
Determined not to lose her stranglehold.
Waiting to pounce when I grow frail and old,
The lines on my face warn me my time is near.

Time is one dimensional, never to be repeated.
She lurks, waiting for my last laboured breath
For me, she is extinguished upon my death.
But time continues, till she finds the next victim.

Despite my fear of her passing away
Time is my precious gift, a commodity
But also a deadly burden, my enemy
With every passing day eating at my soul.

Time is uncontrollable she passes too soon.
Yet she hangs around and won't depart
A grim reaper, tearing at my heart
I try not to waste, but cherish her gifts
But by the time, I've found my way,
She and I are ready to part.

Angela Findlay

I CAN NO LONGER LOVE

I can no longer love,
love's an illusion.
Love present is a spectre
of past image,
to find in one, what I
have lost in another,
apparitions of deceit.

I can no longer love, to
gaze upon some other,
is but to hear, the
phantom voice of lost love,
mock ghostly in the wind,
whispering -
your present love is but a
past corpse.

I can no longer love, love
is a haunting
drowning shadow, beneath
a lake of tears,
tears of despair, despair
born because,
I can no longer love, for
I still love you.

Jos N Ritchie

ROSEBUD

Shy little rosebud
on the brink of maturity
protected by Mother Earth's security
while interred in sodden mud

Covertly enwrapped in gripping sheath
now impatient to unfurl a wreath
of vibrant velvet petals
amid the tangle of thorn and nettles

Sunshine ray and morning dew
both responsible for how she grew
now surging forth in full array
resplendent on a summer's day

Upright now in full-grown bloom
standing tall while others loom
to watch her fall and just decay
her beauty gone, just blown away

Her reign was short but full of hope
now she lies in winter's grope
devoid of colour and lying bare
awaiting the warmth in a mouldy lair.

Assunta Arrighi

A CAMEO

Late April afternoon,
The light of the day half gone
Leaving an afterglow
Across the cloud-streaked sky.
On a slight breeze with salt in it
Small rain comes from a Solway sea fret.
A speckled thrush calls querulously
From the peak of a conifer tree:
'Charley! Charley! Charley!'
'How now. How now. How now?'
'Where? Where?'
Where indeed? There is no answer there;
Although in the distance
A darkling blackbird flutes
Its more melodious song
From some cottage gable.
The light is almost gone,
Even from the bursting maple buds
Turned yellow-green and the bird cherry's
Creamy clusters . . .
As the thrush tries again for:
'Charley. Charley.' Who is not there
So stops to preen his wings, and then
Lifts his tail to void
A quick dismissive squirt,
And flies to roost in the cypress tree.
Apart from the hesitant puttering rain
And a long legged female cranefly
Dancing across the windowpane
Nothing at all - just silence with little light.
No stars as yet.
No moon tonight.

John Parker

THE SWAIN

Now, all the lassies of the village came running out to gawk
At Willie as he passed by to do his daily work.
Now Willie, unbeknownst to all, was very shy with girls,
Brothers, sisters had he none, with whom he could confer.

His trusty steed, old Laddie, his pal and confidant,
Tweaked his ears to listen to Willie's daily rant.
His Ma and Pa were very keen for Willie to be wed,
And from the sale of cattle, had bought the marriage bed.

Willie was a handsome lad, and Laddie knew the one,
The very lass that Ma would like to be wedded to her son.
Her bright blue eyes and auburn hair would suit Willie to a treat
Somehow, old Laddie decided that they would have to meet.

Well the lassies saw them coming, and to the lane they sped
Laddie sensing admiration, proudly tossed his head,
Hooves clattering on cobbles, eye on goal in sight -
He galloped ever onwards pulling cart with all his might.

Willie taken unawares, tried hard to keep his seat,
Sailed through the air to land at Redhead's feet
'Oh Willie,' gasped the lass, 'I've longed so much for this.'
'Marry me,' cried Willie, and sealed it with a kiss.

Wedding day, a shining day, with family, friends around,
Ma and Pa ecstatic with the bride their Willie found,
But no prouder than old Laddie clopping to the Kirk
Bells and brasses shining, garlands round his neck.

Beryl Maxwell

THE RIVER EDEN, APPLEBY

Quiet flows the river
No more wind and rain,
A fish leaps in the silence
And the sky is blue again.

The sun lights up the colours
Of trees in autumn dress,
And leaves drift down so lazily
In response to the wind's caress.

Gracefully they glide along,
Each one a tiny boat,
Making patterns on the water
As down the stream they float.

But now the scene is changing,
Clouds gather in the sky;
Raindrops break the silence
And the leaves are whirled on high.

And so it is along life's way;
We have our ups and downs
And smiles and happy laughter
Can often turn to frowns.

Barbara Kemp

TO LOSE A FRIEND

There comes the day when friends shall leave
Just to move is hard to believe,
To make a new home is quite a task
The best for you is all we ask.
We shall miss you, there is no doubt of that,
Just to meet you and have a little chat.
Helps to pass the working day
That's what friends are for, so they say.

We wish you well in your new home,
With friends and family not far away.
If you need a chat just pick up the phone
Your friends down here are here to stay.

Happy days and pleasant dreams
Are what we wish for you.
So make the most of things to come,
Good luck in your new home.

William Banks

THE RIGHT TO CHOOSE

The dead are cold, soon rotten, buried deep, forgotten
Burned to dust, scattered wide
framed in marble, tarnished pride.
Trapped forever, drowned by tears,
sightless
soundless
formless fears.
A smear upon a time now past, a guilty dent that did not last.
The dead are cold . . .

Life and death are one; then and now are one;
Future past and present, together,
side by side,
a mere stride
between . . .

With death a step away, and thence to life,
what need for strife,
or pain, despair
or blame.
For as we came, so will we go,
our lives, a snail trail, glistening, show
a progression, nothing more,
a game of one with zero score.
To end is but to start, explore
another realm, dimension, perennial flaw.
The only thing we have or are, and cannot lose,
is love,
our keeper, guide and mentor,
and our right to choose.

Bridget Trafford

THE POOR PIGEONS

I am a little pigeon - I live
Right near the bridges
Living on what folks throw away
Chips and half-eaten sandwiches

It's not our fault the mess we make
We're sorry if we spoil it
We've got to do it somewhere
Do you expect us to use a toilet?

The reason that we live in town
There's always a lot to eat
The amount of food that's
Just thrown away - for
Us is a real treat.

If people ate it all - or took
Some of it home, we wouldn't hang
Around - to wait and see what we
Could live on, by finding
It on the ground.

The buildings they protect
Us from this atrocious
Weather, so please don't try
And move us - we don't
Know any better.

Charles Staff

PETALS ON A POOL

How well I remember
the first time we met,
Just a moment in time
I'll never forget.
In solitude, standing
by a small still pool.
'Neath the shade of a tree
so peaceful, and cool.
The scent of wild flowers
wafting on the air,
And a feeling inside
that someone was there.
Gazing into the pool
my heart, leapt a pace.
On seeing reflected,
a man's handsome face.
His smile was quite charming
with warm, loving eyes,
Totally enchanted
I stood, hypnotised.
Alas! Fragrant blossoms
on a soft breeze borne
Disturbed your image
leaving me forlorn.
For there was only me!
A romantic fool,
Weaving dreams around
petals, on a pool.

Patricia Whittle

In Countless Ways

I love you more
than that first cup of tea
or extra five minutes in bed.
More than the taking-off of tight gear
or, 'Next visit to dentist six months ahead.'

More than the smell of onions frying
or satisfying taste of crisp fresh bread
more than lazily lying
cool linen sheets on the bed.
More than Vaughan William's larks skying
over 'Banks of green willow' singing and flying.
In hectic days, more than moments alone
or first glimpse of home after aeons away.
A love through and beyond the spectrum's play
- in poppy red beat of the blood
- marigold glow of early dawning
- daffodil brightness of first spring morning
- or green filtered light through panoplied leaves
- from azure - to Quink-ink blue of the sea
. . . into indigo nocturne of twilight.
To and beyond royal curtain lining 'the end'
Companion . . . carer . . . mentor and friend.

I M Brown

THE PAIN OF BEING BORED

The pain of being bored,
is not like an applaud.

It is like your head is telling you to
do something like making puddings and stew.

It is really a horrible feeling
which I just cannot stand,
the way I am just sitting there
like having my head in the sand.

I get really dizzy
I get very mad
My mind is alarmed
Angry and sad.

With this obnoxious feeling
I start to sigh,
when all of a sudden
my boredom begins to fly.

Bethany Kate Cameron (8)

LOVE OF GOD

I love myself
I love you
I love humanity
I love Him who is the source of all love
Him who is the creator of love
- passion and the educator of the whole world
God is glory, God is great
So you are great
So I am great
My tender lips whisper the sacred words of God
My mouth murmuring drinks the cup of Holy Water
to gain eternal life
For to help and guide stray people
to be the candlelight for the steps of reality and harmless road.

I love myself
I love humanity
I love you
I love Him who is the source of all love
summer comes and goes
and winter pass again
and arrive spring
but the spring of love never passes
never come and go
spring of love is majestic
has got natural beauty
and it is eternal
It's the cause of the happiness in all worlds
so be happy
be tender and eager

be majestic and crown your forehead
with the flower of the spring of love
love of God
love of humanity
and love of yourself.

Ruhi Darakhshani

WHAT NEXT?

What will tomorrow bring?
Another murder, birth or war
Life isn't easy, that's why we break the law
Murder, robbery and stealing cars
Then of course we have the wars
People dying in the third world
All because bombs are hurled
Around the world all goes on
Swindlers are about ready to con
Men are fighting faces are gashed
Cars are stolen, joyrided and smashed
Pensioners are mugged and knocked around
They lie frightened until found
Police are called but nothing is done
The attacker is now out having fun
Punched and kicked hard in the head
Seven weeks in a hospital bed
Leg in plaster and arm in a sling
What else will this bullying bring?
A body of a child is found nearby
The community shocked as they all cry
A child so innocent, no enemies around
We all pray, his murderer is found
All nasty things are still going on
From the rich and famous
To the beggar man's son
These crimes we will stop, if we pull together
Or they'll go on from now till forever.

Lynn Rankin

TOGETHER AGAIN

She looks up at him
From the chair by the fire,
Where he knew she'd be,
Waiting for him.
He feels a sudden surge
Of affection,
For the mother
He hasn't seen
For over fifty years.
No words are spoken,
There is no need,
Forgiveness is in their smiles.
She takes his outstretched hand
And they depart together,
The eternally young leading the old.
In the empty room
Vera Lynn continues to warble
From the gramophone.
She always knew he'd come back,
Mum always knew best.

Clare Anne Lewis

Portrait Of The Alienated

Everyone wears a mask
Everyone wears a mask
Mine is slipping
A chameleon is what I am no more

Always the friend, never the lover

Y'know conforming isn't essential
Wear same clothes,
Same tastes
Hates
It grates on me

You want me to meet and greet
I stare at my feet

Ian Todd

SKIN DEEP

Some say that beauty is only 'skin deep'
And boy does that phrase make me weep
'Cause if you're like me and not blessed with looks
And you spend your time with your head in your books
Your face shouldn't be compared to a mile of bad road
Or look like a lorry that's just shifted its load
You may not have the physique of a Grecian god
All tanned golden brown with a fine rippled bod
Don't feel depressed just hold your head high
Even if inside you feel you should cry
You might have a face only a mother could love
With a complexion compared to a blind welder's glove
Or you could be just plain or a bit overweight
And you're having a hard time attracting a mate
Just don't listen to those who are awful and mean
Suggesting you can't go out 'cause it's not Hallowe'en
Tell them you've never visited the Black Lagoon
And you've never been known to howl at the moon
You're not bothered if you look like ET in specs
You can take all the hurt from those with brass necks
By turning your cheek and ignoring the insults they hurl
You can always remind them even Quasimodo got a girl
But the moral of this story is to play the cards you are dealt
Because being of the facially challenged all these words are heartfelt

Michael Bellerby

FOREST FANTASY

Mists disperse revealing skies
Like strands of grey
Smells of rolling earth and moss permeate the air
Trees' naked boughs twisting and spiralling
A solitary bird squawks in flight
Squirrels, hedgehogs oblivious in their winter bed
Fairy-like trellis patterns on hoar frost ground
A few skeleton brown leaves teased
By chilly winds circle around
Feathery flakes of snow spiral the scene
As I stand surveying this forest fantasy
A message seems to convey
Bleak days of winter
For a while have come to stay.

Sheila Nilsen

ALWAYS LIVE LIKE JESUS

Always be joyful and always be kind,
Like the Lord Jesus who did cure the blind.
For when we are like Him, we live by God's will,
And by loving the Lord Jesus, so God loves us still.
Let us never forget why the Lord lived and died.
He lived as an example, our Good Holy Guide.
And why did He die, on the Hill of Calvary?
Why, He died for us all, so we could always be
Sinless and pure, as pure as the Lord.
Let us never forget Him, but always read His word.
So may we all be like Jesus, and doubt Him never,
Till at last we join Him, to live forever and ever!

Christine M Wilkinson

SWEET DREAMS

If a thought creeps in
To give you a scare
Just call out loud
And I'll be there

For that's what grandads do

I'll sing to you
Old lullabies
Until sweet dreams
Close your eyes

For that's what grandads do
They do
Yes, that's what grandads do

And if a shadow
That stalks the night
Awakens you
With a fright

Just call my name
And I'll be there
With fairy tales
And songs to share

For that's what grandads do

Go to sleep
My bonny bairn
Until the sun
Comes around again

And I shall be
Right by your side
To watch where shapes
And nightmares hide

For that's what grandads do
They do
Yes, that's what grandads do

A I Graham

THE 'INDIAN'

I'm off to eat at the Shish Mahal,
or even the Curry Pot,
I'm very fond of Indian food,
as long as it's not too hot!

Isn't it amazing how,
it appeals to the western taste?
New restaurants springing up each day,
in every little place.

Although we call them 'Indian',
I'm really well aware
Each part of the sub-continent
has its own distinctive fare.
There's Madras curry, Vindaloo,
Chicken Tikka, Poppadums too.
Food from the clay oven
or grilled on a spit,
Naan bread or rice
to go with it.

Samosa parcels,
crispy outside.
Herbs and spices
from far and wide.
All can be got
from the take-away.
Indian food?
It's here to stay!
Once again
I will repeat,
so many people
find it good to eat!

Brian Humphreys

YOU LOVE ME NOT

You have her in your hands
like a pucked flower.

There are depths
you could see there,
as in a rose
fold upon fold of experience
making her what she is.

She could breathe
her particular scent
into your face.

But you are dismembering the petals
until the last one,
when 'he loves me not'
is plain as in a child's game.

Deirdre Armes Smith

THE FOX

The fox
Creeping, cautiously, silently
Its menacing eyes
Its blood-red coat
Its bitter stare.
The fox
Creeping, cautiously, silently.

The fox
Devious, cunning, sly
His impish grin
His crouched legs
His ears pricked for any movement.
The fox
Devious, cunning, sly.

The fox
Mighty, memorable, grand
Its merciless manner
Its well groomed tail
Its proud look
The fox
Mighty, memorable, grand.

Gillian Blake (11)

I MET A GYPSY TODAY

I met a gypsy today
stalking unsuspecting shoppers -
a split second too late
I couldn't escape her gaping eyes -
grasping my hand fiercely
she held me there

embarrassed, harassed,
I wanted to and laughed.

I met a gypsy today
with no pony,
bohemian curls nor heather
she vomited her prophecy, whether
I took heed or not
destiny smiles on the tenth my girl

your girl?

I met two gypsies today
Rosa regurgitated her sisters' tones
holding stones, magic stones
fish tank pebbles of turquoise and peach
£3 each
no, really! thank you!
(your blue jeans and trainers deflate your credibility my girl)

my hand was marred
I wanted to scrub it clean.

I met gypsies today
and I told my mother -
real gypsies are very clean you know
they won't wash underwear
with their
other clothes.

Alexandra Greenwell

THE DEVELOPING SEED

The seed is planted - may soils of life
be fertile and ever loving -
filled with nourishment of life's tapestry
and flower with imaginative beauty.

May the fragrant life have many seasons
and bear fruit of every tomorrow,
there to remain for the joy of others
in gregarious gardens of content.

When autumn shadows lengthen and
withered leaves are feeble with age,
a spirit needs refreshment - like falling rain.
Embryonic life is now death,
while a soul may grow to infinity.

Alex Branthwaite

CLOWNING AROUND

The clown, she's always jolly
You never see her down
Greets you with a great big smile
Not so often a frown
She makes you laugh quite easily
She has the gift no doubt
Behind her smile lays turmoil and fear
And she wants to scream and shout
Tries to be kind and helpful
In so many different ways
Always bright and cheerful
Daft as a brush most days
All the locals know her
Wave and shout hello
Can we walk along with you
You cheer us up you know
But once behind closed doors
The clown just disappears
The mask goes away till another day
She's had the mask for years.

Sandra Witt

ARTHUR WHO?

It's 4.30 in the morning
Just got meself out of bed
Every joint in me body hurts
From me toes to the top of me head
Me feet are worse. Won't hardly move at all
Stumbling about sometimes I fall
Me back is stiff and sore
In fact it's really bad
Me neck, arms and shoulders
What's the score?
The pain is driving me mad
Oh hell, where's the vet to put me down
Out of me miserable state
Then me tablets begin to work
I'm a little better
But not great
Who's this 'fella' Arthur it is
I wish he'd leave me be
Fellas are mostly trouble
And he is yes indeed.

Irene Witte

AUTUMN

Lonely long dark days ahead, the leaves are falling down,
Once so green in colour, now a golden brown,
Days are getting cooler, the sun has lost its heat,
All the birds assemble to make a long retreat.
Just the robin stays with us, he doesn't mind the cold,
As he scratches in the garden, his chest puffed out so bold,
The moon looks cold in colour as it shines there in the sky
The summer has abandoned us, it's time to say goodbye.

Shirley Sucche

HUNGRY BABES

I live far, far away from the real sadness that's around today.
There we live rich and greedy.
But as long as we are full, who cares about the needy?
Hungry children are dying.
Stop and listen, the dear babes are crying.

How immense is the variety of foods we taste.
And we take it all for granted, and waste.
How drastic! In our bin their desire is hurled.
We don't bat an eyelid on the tragedies of this world.
Hungry children are dying.
Stop and listen, the dear babes are crying.

We are all related, can't we save our young?
This will never be, for more centuries sadness is sung.
But there in the future, the one who loves them, he will save,
And feed them many foods to keep them from their graves.
An abundance he will give, like gushing streams.
Tears of joy, the babes will make, they'll be living their dreams!

Kerrie J Dobson

EMERGING FROM THE SHADOW

When you lose a friend, it's a very harsh blow,
You feel that your life is in a black shadow.
But when you lose a close loved one,
You feel that you'll never again see the sun.

You gather once again, family and friends,
Another sombre meeting, it never ends.
A few words from the vicar about Dad's long life,
Pain and suffering over, he's reunited with his wife.

A buffet and a drink, a chat with the lads,
Speaking of memories, about Mum and Dad.
The talking about past events really helps,
The shadows are lightening a bit perhaps.

The one thing that is certain is life goes on,
Memories never die, though the sparkle may have gone.
Positive things can come from tragedy and grief,
Meetings with cousins altogether much too brief.

Looking at mementoes, a hoarder's treasure,
Laughing at memories that you just can't measure.
All of a sudden the shadow is lifted,
Memories of a man, much loved, very gifted.

David Muncaster

SWEETEST FLOWER ON EARTH

Bow down to thee, rose of beauty,
For the glory of your show.
After slumbering all through winter.
Just a few sparse twigs above the snow.
Vigorous you grew and climbing higher
Leaves formed and ripened sun shone gold,
In the light of summer's brilliance
Buds opened as baby's hands unfold.
Petals scrolled like silken pages
Seen in them the sunset's pinkest sky.
Triumphant over all you came through.
Tarnished not by mildew or greenfly.

Strong you grew down through the ages.
Though ever delicate stay your blooms
Long ago Romans adored you
They tenderly laid you on their tombs.
Fade not quickly to decay as the petals down cascade.
Flowering with fragrance so freely made
In full cups perfume, more sweeter than a honey's hive,
And at your display makes it sweeter still to be alive.

May its grace stay in the gardens
Capture its fragrance in meadows,
Grow ever wilder in the hedges
Sweetest flower on earth.

                              The rose.

Susan Bullman

A CHOSEN MAN

I was a chosen man in the Duke of Wellington's campaign,
The soldiers were tired and horses went lame,
The army surgeon splattered with blood after an amputation,
The patient screams in pain with great agitation,
The wounded stagger bleeding their blood red and so bright,
Sabres are slashing reflecting the flashes of sunlight.

I was the regiment sharp shooter accurate and true,
Firing on the enemy dressed in white and royal blue,
The stresses and strains on the soldier's faces,
Long forgotten chivalry manners and good graces,
My powder is low and my shot is all but expired,
My musket did jam as the enemy aimed and fired.

The Frenchman fired his aim was low,
My instant reaction was just far to slow,
The ball hit my chest and knocked me into the sand,
I tried to stop the bleeding with the palm of my hand,
My head is dizzy with the burning pain in my chest,
The blood is oozing out staining my tunic and vest.

As I lay dying who will tell my mother and wife,
And how well I fought when sacrificing my life,
Or the comradeship with the men that I did forge
Bonded together in the support of king George,
I start to shiver and my mouth is parched and numb,
The last thing I heard was the sound of the victory drum.

Bryan Holmes

DIVORCING A TURTLE

I cross the road to hide,
Just to avoid you cos you stood at my side,
I'm battered by the tide
A wreck, exposed
My eyes can not lie
       When I look at you.

Am I haunted by you,
Or are you haunting me?
All I see are debris
Of what you've done to me.

I stuck my neck out
So you gave me a clout,
I'll not do that again
Best to hide, then you can't see my pain.

I'm a wreck exposed
That's just how it goes
Now you see, I know,
You're a plank - your mind is a blank
Like tracing paper,
Now I can not seem to hate her.

She's haunted by me
It's just so dead easy,
And I was a shell
Of my former self,
Now it's her turn on the shelf
It's so dead easy.

You're haunted by me.
I look through you and see
There's nobody in,
You've gone all thin,
All pale 'n' gaunt looking.
You no longer go clubbing,
You're washed up
Done 'n' dusted.
Your hard-nosed exterior
Is all but busted.
So come on,
Stick your neck out.
I'm just in the mood
To give you a clout.

Michael Thompson

REMEMBER ME

You think I've gone away,
Left you to weep by the gravestone,
But forever I will stay,
You will never be alone.

I'll be there when you lie asleep,
To whisper sweet dreams in your ear,
I'll comfort you lovingly while you weep,
For the death of one so dear.

I'll greet you at the crack of dawn,
When the sun emerges from sleep,
And when you're weary and start to yawn,
I'll help you lie down and count sheep.

Don't feel frightened that you'll forget,
The way it used to be,
Take some time at darkening sunset,
To stop and think of me.

In spring the radiant flowers bloom,
In winter, I'll protect you from the cold,
We'll sit together under the autumn moon,
In summer the sun shines, bright and bold.

Now your handkerchief is dry,
Your cheeks are no longer red and hot,
I watch the years pass by,
I plead, forget me not.

Sarah Williams (14)

BONJOUR, MAI!

Flutter by, sweet butterfly, and wave your pretty wings;
Busy bee, accompany the song that each bird sings;
Daisies sparkling in the dewdrops, open to the sky -
Show your lovely faces to the early passers-by;
Gentle breezes, stir the blossoms (frothy, pink and white)
Petals drift, confetti-like: create a bridal sight;
Brooklets in the early sunlight, shimmer as you go:
Lambs and rabbits, gambol in the early morning glow;
Busy cockerel, sound your herald, greet a brand new day;
Skies are bluer now than grey - the summer's on its way.

Rosemary Yvonne Vandeldt

COLD FEET

Here we are, with our quiet little reasons
almost newly wed, already living in different seasons.
Getting to know each other, not well done,
no pleasant mist of romance did reality overcome.
So here we are, looking at our lives,
examining words said and heard one by one.
One by one concealing the painful mental knives.
Truths now between us every time we meet,
you and I, mine and yours, our restless feet.
Our bitter truths souring what once was sweet.
So here we are with all these years ahead,
uneasy thoughts growing, the bitter vine of dread.
Still we must try, endure the little lies,
subduing words that come, ignoring what conscience cries.

G Simpson

BERNHARD'S SHORT BIOGRAPHY

At last Bernhard came to the conclusion
that peace was hibernation to drab death,
that peace was boredom beyond madness,
that peace was like hell without suffering,
that peace was tragedy without events.

So Bernhard deserted his wife and child,
his mistress from not far away Greven;
became a mercenary in some large
African state, boiling with revolutions
and earned himself a few pips for valour.

Today Bernhard is truly contented.
All his future is still well before him.
Every day is like a James Bond film
without cessation and monotony
and each longing is like lust without guilt.

P Krumins

As I Looked Out One Winter's Morn
(Dedicated to Janet Taylor)

'Twas one winter's morn when I beheld
the beauty of an orange tinged sky.
'Twas a morn which held me captivated,
a hazy sun slowly rising upon high.

A frost chilled the air and silence
descended all around.
Not even a bird sang, nor fox or
squirrel disturbed the crystal white ground.

Yet, in the distance, as far as I could see,
I remembered the days we spent together
that were so precious to me.

Then one winter's morn, like the frost
and crystal white gown she had gone.
The sun still rose in the mornings
and I watched it with the arrival of each dawn.
Always keeping those memories of her deep in my heart
forever feeling lovelorn.

Martin Wolff

LUKE'S POEM

Snowflakes flutter by
Twirling, twisting, floating
Robins soon begin to fly
Swooping, singing, swerving.
People toboggan down the hills
Rushing, slipping, sliding.
The cold north wind blows and hisses
Swirling, whirling, cutting.

Luke Spence (7)

MY WORLD

If I ruled the world
Oh, what changes I'd make
There would be plenty of giving
A whole lot less take.

There would be peace in my world
I'd ban all the glue
Teach mothers and fathers
Show them what to do.
My world would be happy
For the young and the old
Little children would learn
To do as they're told.

In my kind of world
All would walk, hear and see
Everyone would be equal
Whatever colour they be.

If I ruled the world
We'd all be the same
No rich man, no poor man
Just one happy chain.

Anne Scrimshaw

DILEMMA

One side shows the logic of
A reasonable attitude to life.
The other, a burning sense of urgency
To fulfil all desires, ambitions, now.

One side says 'bide your time.
Plan and work toward the goal'.
The other demands instant action,
Disregard of caution, self consideration.

One side says 'consider the others,
Protect their interests, before your own'.
The other, 'think of yourself,
They'll be doing the same'.

Through burning conflict, the middle self
Sits on the fence.
Where lies the true path?
There's a tendency to stray.

In times of self assertion, the ways seem down.
In logical pursuance, the journey upwards,
With spirits down, with loathing
Of my smug dullness.

Pauline Boncey

NOCTURN . . .

I tread the leafy woodland path, for sleep deserts my eye,
And restless thoughts keep turning in my head.
The night is still and velvet black, all one the earth and sky.
Yet darker still the hollow where I tread.

A balmy aromatic air perfumes the silent glade,
Evoking thoughts of other nights like this,
Those verdant times of yesteryear, when solemn oaths were made,
Then sanctified with our first stolen kiss!

My senses heightened, now I hear the tinkling of a stream,
Its soothing rhythm calms my fevered brow,
Unending gentle murmurings, where all else is serene,
As on the night we made our lasting vow.

When suddenly, I stand transfixed, to hear the sweetest sound,
For surely only Pan could pipe like this!
Yet hark! A nightingale divine exalts the woods around,
To fill my very heart and soul with bliss.

Were mine the only ears tonight, regaled with ecstasy?
How sad to waste such sweetness on the air,
Or were the spirits of the woods like me,
Enthralled with joy, such rapture we could share?

How glad I am I could not sleep, upon this blessed eve,
Good fortune surely must have borne me here!
For dreams, unlike reality, cannot such magic weave,
Nor opiate drowsing visions can compare.

Leonard Muscroft

THE ANGEL

Silently, by candlelight, he came,
As shadows danced with wild delight,
Soft shadows in nooks and corners
Where cowered the darkness of night.

> Of elfin form, small yet flawless,
> He hovered on hummingbird wings
> Beside the flame, eyes bright and clear,
> Golden head crowned with rainbow rings.

Shimmering auras outward spread
From this angelic, shining boy,
Filling the room with soothing calm,
With love ethereal and joy.

> As early mist in morning sun
> His shape dissolved, drifted away,
> Leaving his essence in the air
> To linger 'til the break of day.

R Smith

VOICES

All day long it's nothing but words:
Never the beautiful song of the birds.

A sweet lass whispering to her new lad:
Others use language that's ever so bad.

A business man clinches a split second deal:
His secretary books an expensive meal.

A doctor is called to a man in great pain:
His dear wife tries very hard to explain.

A school girl's missing - the police are called:
Her parents in tears - the neighbours appalled.

999 to the fire station now:
Then a call to a farmer to catch a lost cow.

Husband calls, *working late yet again:*
His dinner is ruined and wife thinks, *then that's men.*

And so it goes on through the night and the day:
You'd never think they all had to pay.

But whether it's clear or a crackly tone:
I'm the ubiquitous mobile phone.

David Sewell Hawkins

THE THREE SISTERS

We wove a cloak of light and air and dreams.
We linked our arms and whirled and gazed at clouds.
The world outside, existed not for us;
We took its woes and ills, and smiled at them.
Our circle bound us close and hedged our fear;
The chant and cheer of childhood kept us clear
Of age's menace, cynic mind, and slide
To others' grief and deep despair. The spell
We spun is now a threadbare coat, and all
The things we spurned and scoffed are at the door.
Old time's a master not to be denied:
We threw his mirrors and all reminders away,
And thought to stay his loathed advance on us,
But now we know, the debt must now be paid.

Brian MacDonald

OLD FRIENDS

When we heard that Mum had MND the future held no joy
We spoke to experts, read the books, used every means we
                                    could employ
To make her life as pleasant as we possibly could do
But there was nothing to brighten up her days, nothing to look
                                    forward to.
She is more or less confined to home - as we have jobs to go to
Her routine dull and boring - carers, nurses, making do.

But God works in mysterious ways they say and this seems
                                    to be true for her
A friend from her younger days appears, the outlook's exciting,
                                    life is a blur
They go out for walks (well, she's in her chair) he takes her for
                                    trips in the car
To the sea, museums, galleries and shops - love's in the air
                                    and they never stop!

It makes me feel so grateful that she's been given this wonderful chance
At 76 who could expect new love their life to enhance
So no matter how much time is left, love has changed her life you see
I thank God with all of my heart for her - she's not yet been
                                    beaten by MND.

Maureen Seymour

ANDREW, WITHOUT YOU

Without you in my life
Pancake day wouldn't happen two days of the year,
Classic FM would play music that I couldn't hear,
There wouldn't be picnics in Clumber Park,
I'd spend my Saturdays playing gooseberry to Jane and Mark.

Without you in my life
The cinema would only show films in black and white,
Stephen King could no longer give me sleepless nights,
I'd not be a local in the Skellow Grange,
And I would actually miss that, though I find it strange.

Without you in my life
My mobile would sleep silent at 2am,
I'd not know the lyrics to songs by Eminem,
I wouldn't ride pirate ships or mechanical birds,
I'd read the great poets but not feel their words.

Without you in my life,
Andrew, it's incomplete,
I know that the two of us were destined to meet,
You've made me so happy, this poem cannot say,
I'll be grateful forever that we met on that day.

Jody Richardson

WHEN YOUNG LOVE STONES DUMB YOUR BRAIN

When young love stones dumb your brain
With one nippled drug, my son
Be quick to push for the second touch,
For only love is another man's loss
Rehearsed to moisten the breast
Lies robbed, is ready to drop
Where youth shares more of love's dose.

Quell all love's shapely tastes -
Staying dry to youth's bent curves
Shall calm in common play -
Worry not for love's great age:
Let young blood stone dumb your brain.

Jason B Robinson

SENSING

When you are not inside our home
My heart tells me you're not alone
For in my heart I sense you there
Upstairs, downstairs, everywhere
As I wander, room to room
I catch a smell of your perfume
I see the chair in which you rest
Hear your voice begin to jest
Then my heart begins to pound
I hear your footsteps on the ground
My life is full again, once more
For you are walking through the door.

James Eden

ONE UPMANSHIP

The Jones' and Smithson's were rivals,
Good neighbours? No, certainly not,
Whatever the Smithson's had purchased,
The Jones' had already got.

Their rivalry lasted for ages,
They bettered each other for years,
They died within months of each other,
The end, you think, so it appears.

Yet even in death they were feuding
As their graves were laid side by side,
The folk of the village were happy,
The day that these two couples died.

One night though, a storm hit the graveyard,
The lightning was flashing around,
It struck the headstone of the Jones'
And caused it to crack and lay down.

The vicar was most disappointed,
So off to the council he went,
He told of the storm in the parish
And of how the gravestone was leant.

Some workmen arrived in the morning,
Decided the stone was no good
And until another was purchased
They'd made it as safe as they could.

They got some strong wire and a fence post,
Then tied up the offending stone,
It once again stood nearly upright,
At teatime the workmen went home.

That evening the Smithson's were strolling
At midnight, like all spirits do,
When they spied the Jones' old headstone,
Ma Smithson said, 'That wire is new'.

'Well would you believe it,' said hubby,
As every expletive he called,
'They've really outdone us with this love,
They've had a telephone installed.'

John Conquest

COMPUTING

Computing is the thing to learn for young and old alike
To write, to add, or just play games
It gives you something to do each day
Games by the hundreds you can see, more for the children not for me
I prefer to have a try, and keep up to date with all events
Of birthdays, anniversaries and holidays, that occur in the family
Spreadsheets help us with our bills, to see on screen at a glance
Whether or not you have the chance, to keep on spending or hold back
Until your cash flow is back on track

Audrey Allott

WALKING HOME FROM THE VET'S SURGERY

How many people passing me by
See the tears well in my eyes,
How many people sense my grief
Beneath my dabbing handkerchief,
Who notices in the rush hour race
The look of sorrow on my face.

Now heavy in my aching arms
Remembering those endearing charms,
Walking home I say a prayer
For the lifeless bundle cradled there.

Christine A Lee

TO BE OR NOT TO BE

I'm tired of toiling, and striving, and struggling.
I wish I was a *cat*.
The one of course, that gets the cream.
But I'm allergic to fur, so would be sneezing and wheezing
And that state of affairs I would not find pleasing,
No matter, I'll be a *bat*.

An uninvited guest at all weddings and christenings
Gazing at Bonnie Babies and Beautiful Brides.
But I've thought of a snag, bats hang upside down,
Now that would make me dizzy.
So reluctantly I'll give that a miss,
And contemplate being a *hat*.

A bowler, a Stetson, or a bright Easter bonnet,
Atop a blonde cloud of curls.
But as fashion is fickle, I would soon be a *hat* been!
Unloved and unworn, replaced at the drop of a cap!
So I'll turn up my brim at that idea,
And think about becoming a *mat*.

I could be a cosy fireside rug,
Handy for watching TV.
But what if I was only by the front door?
People wiping their shoes all over me!
I couldn't stand that, so I'll try again,
Instead I'll be a *gnat*.

I would be able to bite someone I don't like,
If they had been horrid to me.
But that's not my nature, I'm not really mean
If the truth is known, I'm really just keen to tootle along as before.
So when all's said and done, I really should settle,
Just for being me!

Cherry Kipling

PESTILENCE

A cry goes out in a North Yorkshire farm,
The farmer's livestock has come to harm.
His cows have got the foot and mouth,
Which, very quickly, spreads to the south.

How did it find its way to Devon?
They hold out hands and look to Heaven.
Modern farming could hold the key,
It seems we have to wait and see.

Pigs and sheep can't escape the cull,
Disease don't favour just the bull.
Funeral pyres light the winter sky,
Acrid smells from byre and sty.

Rural businesses go up in smoke,
Gone are the dreams of country folk.
No more do the tourists come to stay,
They are just sad memories of yesterday.

It stops the pest in 'four by four',
Spreading virus from door to door.
Gorging ruts in rural lane,
Causing farmers constant pain.

The bad news comes from o'er the water,
That foreign lands must do their slaughter.
Vet zooms down on farm and heath,
And panic follows the merchant of death.

So, pray to the God of Heaven and Earth,
That science can end this awful curse.
This plague which sweeps across the land,
The timer is running out of sand.

William Knapton

WHEN I GO

I went to a funeral the other day
And I started to think this isn't the way
I want things when it happens to me.
I want flowers and colours and plenty of songs.
No black clothes, glum hymns and funeral gongs.

If I die early I'll be most annoyed
The idea of long life is with what I have toyed
So if I go soon I'll be cross.
I would like my picture upon a wall
Then maybe I can join in with it all.

I don't want a vicar with ashes and dust
But family or friend to stand up and just
Talk of the life I have lead.
Don't bury me yet until all has been told
And colour my coffin with ribbons so bold.

I think flashing lights would be over the top
But let spirits flow and let good wine slop
And all have a jolly good feast.
Then on a warm summer night leave your windows ajar
And say, 'Look Grandma Stella's a star.'

Stella M Taswell

THE BECKONING HILLS

Come away with me to the purple hills
And the moors all covered with heather,
Let us see ere we die
Where the wild birds cry
Then fly off with a flip of a feather.

There's a place I know, where winds sweet and fresh
Blow softly a murmuring prayer,
We can dream as we climb
From the dull city grime
For dreams seem much closer up there.

Come away from the roads and petrol fumes
Let the world and his wife rush on by,
We can walk and talk
Where the plover and hawk
Will not mind if we hold hands and sigh.

Towns are all hurry and scurry and rush
There's no time to stand still and stare,
Passers-by grimly nod
One would really think God
Gave them nothing but heartache and care.

Come away to the hills where lambs leap and play
And wild rabbits scuttle and hop,
Some tors are so high
That their crowns touch the sky
And the clouds seem to rest on the top.

Life is so short and each passing day
Is a day that will soon be gone,
But yesterday's dreams
Near cool moorland streams
Will stay in our hearts and live on.

P M Parlour

A SUMMER ROMANCE

When winter comes and hoar frost paints the trees,
And far off hills become December-misted,
I will remember this summer and the gentle breeze,
Which sighed and moaned, and softly whispered!
We sat beneath the willow tree,
And watched the river rippling by,
We made a vow; to stay together,
And spoke of love which never dies,
The earth and sky, and flowers and rain,
Are part of love's sweet tapestry,
How could we know there would be pain?
When summer died and autumn came!
When the leaves fell from the willow tree,
Our love died too - then came the rain,
It swelled the streams, it filled the river,
It drenched my soul with tears and pain,
When far off hills became April-misted,
And snowdrops bloom, and the old sun,
Red and rosy after his winter's sleep,
Wakes; and warms the Earth again,
Then love may return, in all its beauty,
And give me hope, and dreams again.

Betty Wildsmith

SKY DAYS

Reach for the sky,
And make a big smile,
Open your heart and let love run wild,
Don't go to the bottom,
Go to the top above the clouds,
See it more clearly,
The light blue colour mixed with white,
Floating like cotton wool puffy and huge,
You can dream of being on a cloud,
Like being on an island,
Island of paradise,
Where no problems or worries,
Just you alone with the clouds,
What dreams, what life, what love and happiness,
Those are the days, the sky days.

Sandra Pickering

A LADY I LOVE

There is a lady in my life
Who has strength, charisma and charm,
A kindness that is unsurpassed,
And personality so wonderfully warm,
She has silver hair and lovely skin
It puts my own to shame!
A hard life she's had
And stood up to it well.
I think 'courage' is her middle name!
She's taken some 'knocks' and comes bouncing back
Each and every time!
Yes I'm speaking of my dearest friend,
That wonderful mother of mine.

Patricia Marie Walters

A DREAM

Into the cave I walked alone,
A shiver went down my spine,
I wished I wasn't on my own,
But with my loving canine.

The air was chill,
The temperature low,
Animals out for the kill.
I dare not move or make a sound,
I tried to keep so still.

The cave was dark,
The air was damp,
Strange noises filled my ears,
I wished that I had got a lamp
To chase away my fears.

My fear of darkness ever growing,
Thoughts of things in the night,
Filled my mind with not knowing
If it would ever be light.

Then I felt a terrible bump
And let out a piercing scream,
I felt my head, there was a lump,
But it woke me from my dream.

K S Hackleton

THE LURE OF THE RIVER

A riverbank, so quiet and still,
The line and float in place.
A tired man rests his eyes
And his mind.

Here in this world there's tranquillity and peace
Time passes and with it his cares.
The heart of the river is open and calling,
Its soul, to him, laid bare.

It ripples and flows and gently winds,
Its path ageless, unchanged by time.
Away with the flow go his worries.
He smiles,
There's a fish on the end of his line.

Janet Munnings

A SPECIAL PERSON

My mam is not of great stature
In fact she's not very tall
She's only about 4'10"
So! really she's quite small
Her voice can be big and boom like a drum
To hear her voice sounds like she's 6'1"
Her commanding tone makes you jump to your feet
Sometimes she can be really sweet
Kind and generous to a fault, yes sir!
But! be warned if you take advantage of her
She may be disabled and not walk very well
But! her brain is in tact, she can put you through hell
Does not suffer fools very gladly
From experience I speak
Gives a certain look which means don't speak
'Always' she's been houseproud, still is at 74
When things are done wrong, chucks me out the door
Always impatient, her temper rises in a flash
Then 'we' all disappear, sorry must dash
Has a good sense of fun when not in pain
And can make you laugh again and again and again
'Always' she's worked hard, 48 hours a day
Expects us to be just the same way.
But she's my mam and I love her you see
Cos! She's leaving all her money to me
Always it's a special time for her and me
I put up with her and she puts up with me
I consider her age and the things she's had wrong
So somehow we seem to get along.

G H Whit

GOD'S VALLEY

There's a valley in the Green Hills
called the Valley Of The Moon,
where silver light embalms the trees
and banishes all gloom.
I wandered in that moonlit glade
in my youth and in my prime,
beside the silver chattering stream
my star was in its trine.
When sunshine filtered through the trees
and dappled all around,
in the stillness of that verdant vale
the peace of God I found.

In the quiet of that valley
when the sun has gone to rest,
when the birds have ceased their calling
and settled in their nest,
when the silent silver moonshine
casts pale shadows 'neath the trees,
the love of God surrounds me
in the soft, warm, evening breeze.
Whispering trees invite me
to taste God's precious love.
It reaches me through distant space
from far away above.

'Though I have wandered far and wide
and left my native land,
in dreams I travel back again
to where the tall trees stand.
I see the moon-made shadows
of the trees beside the stream
and I see that moon reflected
on the water in my dream.
God's gentle voices drive away
all misery and gloom;
His loving arms surround me
in that Valley Of The Moon.

John S Bertram

IMAGINATION

I left the cinema one evening,
After watching a scary film,
I felt very uneasy,
And was still shaking within.

I walked down a dimly lit alley,
As this was my only route home,
I sensed a kind of presence,
Even though I was quite alone.

The hairs stood up on the back of my neck,
As this eeriness gave me the creeps,
And far away in the distance,
I could hear someone else's feet.

My heart started to thump faster,
The sweat just poured from my brow,
I came to a sudden standstill,
And knew my end had come now.

I felt a hand on my shoulder,
I turned cold and then white,
My mouth hung open in terror,
And my eyes stuck out in fright.

I turned around very slowly,
Expecting to meet my end,
And saw Pete my next door neighbour,
Whom until now, thought was a friend.

Antonina Hardy

UNTITLED

(Dedicated to Valerie Anne 1937-1993)

Cancer is ugly, cancer is death,
And it strikes when we least expect it,
Cancer is the eater of body, mind and soul,
Devouring us all inside,
Cancer is that pain and grief,
Leaving behind the bereaved,
Trying to find a way to cope,
And trying to find a new hope,
For cancer is one of the ultimate killers,
In today's society.

And I will never forget that day in '93,
When cancer took you away from me,
Destroying our family,
And a day has never gone by -
Without me thinking of you Mother,
And I thank you for all the love you gave,
Even thou' I was the black sheep of the family
You still loved us all the same
And finally this is to say -
Thank you for being there through -
All the good and bad times
And that you're always in my thoughts and heart.

Martyn Leigh-James

LIFE LESSONS

And, through eternity
we came through.
Many lives we have
battled through.

And through this life
as before.
Gathered momentum
to reach our goal.

In our hearts
we both know

what will come
and what will go . . .

To finally rest
on some peaceful shore

all of life's lessons
learnt once more.

Tracy Hopkins

LOOKING BACK

The woods and fields with streams and flowers
where I spent many happy hours,
are just a memory, growing dim,
of a different time that I've lived in.
Then, life was slower, and simpler too
with many interesting things to do.
Houses sit on fields where once I played,
the flowers I picked - the daisy chains I made.
Gentle horses lived there then -
around the time that I was ten.
The stream that bubbled, clear and bright,
now looks a most depressing sight,
all choked with weeds, too weak to flow,
why must those happy child years go?
The woods long gone where once I roamed at ease,
'Make way for progress' - cut down the trees.

Margaret Whitton

YOU SEND ME FLOWERS

My life had no meaning
until you came along
you accepted me
for who I was

You didn't care about
my past but you
cared that I'd been hurt
and that in turn hurt you

You shower me with
your love and understanding
give me my own space
encouraging me to do
all the things I feel
I need to do
you are my best friend

Sometimes I would hurt you
for no reason at all
then I would see the hurt
in your eyes and I would
feel remorse

Why do I hurt you
time after time
when you have brought
something unique and
wonderful into my life

But you always forgive me
in your thoughtful and
considerate way and
send me flowers.

Kath Gabbitas

SEASIDE HOLIDAY 1950

Clickity click! Clickity clack!
The steam train is rushing along the track
Heather and I and Mum and Dad
All so happy, all so glad.

A fortnight's holiday by the sea,
I feel the sea is just waiting for me!
The sun always shone, or so it seemed
It probably rained! It probably teemed!

We had buckets and spades to build sandcastles high
Kites that soared and really wanted to fly!
Ices and rock and candyfloss,
Our few pennies were never at a loss!

Saved and worked for all year round,
Just to tread some sandy ground,
Paddling with Dad at the edge of the sea
We giggled at him with trousers rolled to the knee.

Smells of chips and salty sea
Mingle with pop and a nice cup of tea.
Donkey rides too were such a treat,
With furry coats against our feet.

All long gone now as the steaming train
Never to return for me, quite the same,
A generation has now moved on,
It's my children now taking their children along.

Patricia Packer

MUM

There she stands all in a fluster
'Where've I put my yellow duster?'
Oh there it is you silly moo
It's in my hand, the polish too

Her memory is a bit misty today
Forgot to put the dishes away
Next time I'll write a list she says
My memory isn't that good these days

With a cheery face and roar of laughter
She loves a joke there's no denying
I'll have to do some ironing
So much work it's very tiring

What is this ache I have today?
Too much walking yesterday
'Don't worry,' says Dad, 'it will go away
Just do as I do, it will be okay,
Light a fag and read all day.

Shout at the men on the telly
Go on Mam, give him some welly!'

Jacqui Beeston

THE MIRACLE OF SNOW

Snowy-white petals coming down
Children smile, adults just frown
Sliding all over the place
Or a good snowball chase
Snowmen being built as large as can be
All built up, smiling happily
Snow can be enjoyed on wintry days
As it falls it trips and sways
It comes to the ground so gentle you see
As it comes down so vast and furiously
Snow is pure white
Snow is a beautiful sight
I loved to slide all over the place
Going downhill with good grace
Today when I am looking out
Something in me gives a shout
Snow is falling, swaying with glee
Yes snow is a mystery
Snow has come again today
The children all shout hip, hip, hooray
Snow can be a rewarding treat
Playing out in the local street

Irene Holden

WHAT IS LIFE?

What is this thing called life?
To some it's trouble and strife,
Others find it monotonous and dull,
While some live it to the full.

Life to everyone is sweet,
Each day a new challenge to meet,
But sometimes we have a really good day,
Then we can conquer anything come what may.

There are people who are never content,
Others who don't intend to pay the rent,
Some even make their lives such a mess,
Don't know how to make things right I guess.

Do we all know what we seek?
Are some of us far too meek?
Is ambition the true key?
Or are we content to let things be?

Myself I live day to day,
Make the best of what I've got some say,
Some just look for something to blame,
Maybe it's to hide some shame.

Pamela Earl

THROUGH THE EYES OF A CHILD

If we could see the world through a child's eyes
We would see a wondrous sight
Without violence, or fear, no tantrums or tears
Just a place to please and delight.

If we could see into the mind of a little child
We would see all the good things in store
Oceans of love, skies of blue
Happiness behind every door.

It just maybe only make believe
Where even heaven is a house up in the sky
And little angels act as playmates
While Jesus gently passes by.

Don't ever take away a child's dream
Reality ebbs back like a tide
Yet for a little while all you see are smiles
If you see the world through the eyes of a child.

Vera Ewers

HUSBAND'S LOVE
(Dedicated to Peter with my love)

I've been out of action
For twelve weeks or more.
I've not had to cook the meals
Or sweep the kitchen floor.

For I took my son John fishing,
And I fell down, oh heck!
I went and broke my hip again,
Oh heck! Oh heck! Oh heck!

I was hurried off to hospital
As fast as it could be,
To get myself patched up again,
Poor me! Poor me! Poor me!

Home I came on crutches,
Happy but feeling lame.
My husband said, 'Now Madam
No fishing for you again!'

He's nursed me and helped me
Along this painful road.
He's bathed me and fed me,
And carried all the load.

The shopping and the cleaning,
The garden work as well.
He's never complained, oh no, not him,
He really was so swell.

Now I'm feeling better
And I'm getting strong again
I will resume all the chores
And never will complain.

For I thank God I'm mended
With screws and plates and things,
And my dear husband Peter was there for me,
To me that's everything.

Kathy French

TIME'S LEGACY

... the erosion of memories until there is no one
left to remember.

Claimed by *time,* elegance and grandeur
collapse into neglect, forsaken in ruin and decay.
Ghastly, odious, the legacy of time,
yet possessed with a beauty all its own.

Through derelict, stained-glass windows,
dust motes, like music notes, hover on sunlight shafts.
Shadows, small, tall, lurch from pillar to wall.
Under weather-worn arches marches
a regiment of forgotten souls,
restless in the gloom of a sombre, eroding tomb.
In old, bold cracks in the dirty, flagged floor
woodlice and mice forage midst the debris of time.
Disintegrating pews, once grand, black now, grim,
decay odorous and deep within.
Big black birds prance in a ritual dance of gorging, gouging,
hideous and cruel in an orgy of clamour.
From beams of a rotten slate roof,
creaks and squeaks cross the quiet,
straining, settling, wheezing, easing - an old man's chest.

Wendy Gledhill

A CERTAIN SOMETHING!

I checked my mirror image;
before leaving for the shops.
Quite pleased with my appearance,
I'd pulled out all the stops.

I glided, poised and elegant,
along the concrete pathway.
A certain air of savour-faire,
made me feel so chic, so stately.

The people passing gasped in awe,
my appearance must have startled.
How stunning I must look to them,
but some of them just chortled.

How rude I thought and gave each one,
a rather haughty glare.
How ignorant and very rude,
they should know better than to stare.

On passing by the shop's window,
I took a sideward peek
and open-mouthed I now did see
what they'd seen in the street.

I'd only checked my frontal view,
I should have checked the back;
my skirt hem tucked up round my waist,
was what made their jaws go slack.

So check from every angle girls,
let my story warn of errors.
There's nothing spoils your chic-ness more,
than flashing your old knickers!

Patricia Pearson

A Soldier's Regret

The moon dipped into the frosty horizon
Its shadowed light reflecting in the smouldering air
A gaseous atmosphere, lingering,
Covering the dormant village.
Children, once playful and endearing, dying.
Their bodies reflecting the degradation of war.
The bicycle, twisted, manacled,
Half standing in defiance, unwilling to buckle.
The dog, jaded by malnutrition, whimpered
As it cowered before the dismantled door,
Its frightened frame was too weak to suggest its hunger.
The veterinarian's corpse
flightless, breathless, caged.
The cauterised street sheds its silence
Allowing the unhinged door to creak its discontent.
The murmuring of the hidden wounded
Clearly heard yet undefined.
The remnants of a ravished village
Could not abnegate the silhouette
Of victorious misery;
And defeat in a battle won.

Pam Reynolds

HOLISTIC HARROGATE

A ridge of disturbance,
Volcanic upheaval,
As springs percolated,
Platonic waters rose.

Carboniferous layers,
Produced mineral waters,
Strangers to daylight,
From the darker regions.

Giving birth to the cures,
From a volcanic bed,
A free gift of nature,
Born out of turbulence.

Elegant buildings, spa,
Royal baths and pump room,
With doctors to advise
On contents of treatments.

Waters from furnaces,
Rages from cooled and calmed,
From a chaos long past,
Harnessed for benefit.

Kathleen Mary Scatchard

DUNKIRK

Noon.
The sun is over the yard-arm
And who hears the clarion-call
- the distant boom -
The sun, splendid, high overhead:
Where numerous voices in taverns
Pay homage to the dead.
Sup ale, toast in some far distant room
And talk of 'how it would be over soon'.
Talk randomly, dreamily, of what wise men have read
. . . somewhere . . .
And slumbers, deep where whispers fall, to
Leave grey ghosts in the memory of recall.
Grey faces in dawn
Split atoms:
While someone, somewhere
Plays croquet on a velvet lawn.

P J Harris

WORKING MAN

Stone on stone, attempting balance. Always looking for
enclosure and the straight edge. These are carcass stones
with the moss stripped and discarded. Skinned and rough
bodied to stain his hand. Stone friends, expecting nothing.

He is rebuilding and making good. Putting back the lines
to hold a landscape. He is medieval, all monked
and hooded against the rain. He is becoming history.
A quiet history, easy to forget. He listens to the stones

and their endless, dull stories of death under the sea.
They have treasures now uncovered; an adder skin, two
grass cups for nests, a yellow sheep skull. He will take
them as presents for an occasional nephew. Later air blasts

off the high ridge and blows bracken scraps down the
valley. The rain slants across to turn the sheep. Their
fleeces shiver and part like dirty waves. They watch him
unconcerned as ever. He stretches and yawns at the fast

unfastening clouds. Then firms a last stone and slow walks
down the evening to a quiet house. Stone man in the rain.

Joanne Benford

THE LAKES

I want to go to the lakes again,
To the lonely tarns on high,
To Castlerigg and Aulde Meg,
And to see an eagle fly.

I want to paint a mountain
With small clouds floating by
In rich viridian greens,
And an ultramarine sky.

With easel, stool and rucksack,
I'll walk over hills and farms,
In search of new locations
That offer me their charms.

And when I've finished painting
And the sun finds time to rest,
There'll be another dawn
For me to do my best.

Margaret Sanderson

POSSIBILITIES

Close your eyes . . . what do you see?
Blackness.
Look beyond the blackness and your eyes will truly open.
You will be dazzled by an array of colours,
Colours that reality cannot bleed.
Colours that are mixed inside you, they need no
Solid form to show off their beauty.
They bleed together engulfing your thoughts
And possessing your dreams.
If you stop searching your colours will
Harden and your reality will die.
You can fuel new concepts, change the way
People think and perceive.
Endless creative journeys to travel and experience.
Anything is possible.
Tomorrow is another story, make it happen
And keep it.
That's the power of imagination.

Luke Forster

FALLING IN LOVE

Every day is summer in my heart
My face beams like the sun
The blue sky shines brightly within my eyes
My life is full of fun

Each day brings happiness and joy
Since that moment when we met
Not showing him my true feelings
Is the only thing I regret

I daydream about him constantly
I keep hearing bluebirds sing
There's not one day that goes by
When I imagine wearing his ring.

Christine Robinson

DIAGRAM

Drawing a delicate exquisite
admirable style skilful and ingenious,
the lyric pirouettes
at the ceilidh.
The crescendo and credence
discern the crystal
and bauble.
The distinctive aroma
laces the pimpernel and lupin
with extreme beauty.

Turning the courteous
sumptuous expert bedecked
in charming apparel
spins and curves,
confidence excellently
matchless.
Pendulous delicious
fastidious commendations
fashion and honour
the plane surfaces.

Flakes laminate,
added by chance
to decorate and
drape the elegant robes.
The esteem and standing
graciously accomplish
the customary niceties.

Sarah Margaret Munro

TO MAM

To mam I love you so
I just want you to know
whatever I do
whatever I say
I'll always love you every single day.

You are like a best friend to me
if you weren't here I don't know where I would be
so whatever I do
whatever I say
I'll always love you every single day.

Thanks for caring
thanks for sharing
thanks for looking out for me
'cause without you here I don't know where I would be.

Aimee Upton (15)

COLD MOURNING

The cold morning calls me,
And I wake, solemnly.
A dying cat mews in my head,
As I gently rub my eyes
Cockroaches scurry across my skin
And nip at my fingers and toes.
The bubbly night dissolves in my mind
And my cotton wool tongue lays limp.
Last night - what a night,
Someone's birthday, I vaguely recall.
Beside me she sleeps,
Sweet slumber for my dearest.
I remember we danced through the streets
Flamenco, lambada, samba, rumba - we did them all
It's amazing what you do after a drink.
Wait, who was that girl?
Her sweet blonde hair reached down below her waist,
And her blue eyes shone into my soul
Stirring feelings I've not felt since . . .

Peter Davey

PRIDE - 7 SINS

Patience is a virtue
Pride won't allow
Erratic sandbags
Thrown around the wall

Prevarication prevails
O' cursed contradiction
Loitering non-intent
In case of a conviction

Saintly on reflection
Listens unreadily
Seven different reasons
One sin so deadly.

Gillian Day Trainer

BROTHERS

Brothers are friends and that's for life,
Brothers are friends all the time,
They play and learn and teach each other things,
And love being with each other and all the love it brings.

We have three children, three boys
And that's how we know the happiness and joys
That three boys can give in return,
Brothers together, brothers for life,
Brothers forever, friends in return.

Love is a gift that can grow with them in time,
And love for each other will forever shine.
As we watch them grow each day,
We know in our hearts they'll show each other the way,
Brothers forever and a day.

Lorraine Dignen

WINDOW LIFE

I built this fear and paranoia myself
to protect my state of mind.
I cower at my window and coldly survey all that has been taken
away from me, forced or otherwise.
False tears flow freely down my plastic face as in remembrance
to my friends the strangers in the street.
It might be the painfully thin old man with the constant
phlegm-filled cough, the arthritis in his bony hands so painful.
He has to be spoon-fed by a bored teenage girl who falsely
thinks she has charity in her heart.
As she walks by the window she desperately dreams of leaving
the smell of old age and death behind her.
The gleam from her tacky gold jewellery blinds my eyes
but I still notice that her stomach is tightly swollen with the
tracksuit generation.
I shudder at this thought and the havoc it may wreak.
Her baggy jeaned-arse leaves my line of sight
and again as if on cue the tears come but this time I can
taste the bitter salt on my lips.
My heart secretly yearns for the life on the other side of the glass,
then the rain comes and brings me a friend.
A woman elegantly dressed in black scampers past,
her face absent due to her umbrella.
A smile tries to decorate my face but is soon dismissed
as some form of life begins again.

Keith Horsley

CONSOLATION

I fail to see the reason why
A maiden weeps, a man will sigh,
Because their sun goes down behind a hill.
If they cried a hundred years,
And they shed a million tears
The sun keeps going down, it always will.

But one thing that I know,
And this I tell them so,
Don't waste precious time on fruitless sorrow.
Be thankful for the night,
It makes your love shine bright,
And your sun will rise again on you tomorrow

N Magee

GFS

Galley's Field School of great renown,
Set against the town moor,
The athenaeum of the town,
Known as the best of Hartlepool's schools,
No time at all for idiots or fools,
Once through the gates no larking about,
Get sat down and writing books out,
Learning the three Rs was the school's main aim,
And always to remember to play up and play the game,
So when the time comes to leave this school,
And go forth into the world, from historic Hartlepool,
To always remember to say, 'I know I can',
I went to Galley's Field School,
Where I was taught to be a gentleman.

Ted

THE OTHER SIDE

This child stood in little more than rags,
with holes in shoe
socks dirty, visible.
Her greasy yellow hair
looked stained with nicotine.

In envy she stood watching
while clean children played,
the black rings beneath her blue eyes
peered into the park, through the wrought iron gate.

This was a world away
where all her dreams awoke to reality,
she watched the other children play on the slide
against her look of sadness,
seeing a mother comforting her baby which cried.

I watched her eyes wishing time after time
to be on the other side of the gate,
but often, I would see her there alone,
sitting on the swings in the rain.

She came every day that summer
wishing she would be asked to play,
but she was never noticed
only by me, who missed her yesterday.

C Leith

A Sound Scientific Explanation Or Two

Soft silent silence sound.
Low pressure destroying.
High pressure shrieking.
Equilibrium seeking.
Only a wanton wilful wind.

Different atomic vibrations.
Different aural perceptions.
Oilrig divers' deceptions.
Helium causing voice alterations.
Only a voice emasculating gas.

Modern massive microwave measuring saucers
interfering with outer space.
Neighbours interfering.
Cutting calm.
Only a musical megablaster.

Sound animated dancers
wearing over - well-washed jeans.
Sound intelligence,
intents and health.
Only a matter of genes.

K Chesney-Woods

NATALIE

I was hypnotised,
I was mesmerised,
By her caryatid bellvadeor,
Her inextricable pulchritude,
The abnegating impetus
Of her columbine countenance,
Such efficacious philtre
Of my dilettante acquisitiveness,
Her augmentative beaxart
Of exiguous epithet,
Demulcent to her visceral
Paean of sagacious philoxenia,
Devoted thus I to the integral
Of her fecund albedo.

Anthony John Ward

ANCHOR BOOKS
SUBMISSIONS INVITED
SOMETHING FOR EVERYONE

ANCHOR BOOKS GEN - Any subject, light-hearted clean fun, nothing unprintable please.

THE OPPOSITE SEX - Have your say on the opposite gender. Do they drive you mad or can we co-exist in harmony?

THE NATURAL WORLD - Are we destroying the world around us? What should we do to preserve the beauty and the future of our planet - you decide!

All poems no longer than 30 lines.
Always welcome! No fee!
Plus cash prizes to be won!

Mark your envelope (eg *The Natural World)*
And send to:
Anchor Books
Remus House, Coltsfoot Drive
Peterborough, PE2 9JX

OVER £10,000 IN POETRY PRIZES
TO BE WON!

Send an SAE for details on our New Year 2001 competition!